THE MILKCRATE MONOLOGUES VOL.1:

HIPHOP MONOLOGUES FOR THEATRE

BY **RON JOHNSON JR.**

To request permissions, contact the author at
estronemicas@gmail.com or call
(831) 623-5280 or 301 The Alameda
Suite 532, San Juan Bautista, CA 95045.

Paperback ISBN: 978-1-66780-506-1
E-book ISBN: 978-1-66780-507-8
Audiobook ISBN: Digital 978-1-66792-996-5
Digital Library 978-1-66792-997-2

Library of Congress Control Number:
2021921151

The Milkcrate Monologues: Hiphop Monologues for Theatre was made possible through the generosity of Bess Foster Bronson, Rose Andom, Ronald W. Johnson, Sr, Nancy Cheryll Davis-Bellamy, Andrew Ceglio, Melissa Booey, Michael Duarte, Sebastian Huerta, Demone Carter, Lilia Agüero, FutureArtsNow!, the School of Arts and Culture, Towne Street Theatre, Zoot Suit Productions.

This book is a production of Estronemicas D.M.R. We are an independent production company specializing in the performing arts, digital media, and arts education. Founded in 2010 by Ron W. Johnson Jr. in partnership with Estrella Esparza-Johnson and longtime collaborator, Andrew Ceglio to harness their skills and experiences as writers, playwrights, screenwriters, producers, actors, directors, video editors and teledramatic artists and performers. We create and practice a high caliber dramatic art influenced by Hiphop culture and the American experience.

We are comprised of two divisions: *Arts Education* and *Professional Services*. Our arts education division contracts with educational organizations and partners to provide dramatic arts teaching artist services to students from kindergarten through 12th grade as well as adults. Our professional services division provides acting, play - and screenwriting services, live theatrical, media and entertainment producing and marketing, directing, music composition, production, and musician services.

We are on a mission to foster, create and share our unique American stories, our *Dreams Made Reality.*

THE MILKCRATE MONOLOGUES VOL.1

INTRODUCTIONS

It was in the Fall of 2013 that Ron Johnson joined the faculty of the School of Arts and Culture as the instructor for a new course titled: HipHop Theater. Ron brought a deep appreciation for the parallels among the themes, language and cadence of Hiphop - and that of Shakespeare's poetry. But it was his artistry and honesty as a Rapper and Actor combined with an ability to feel young people in their process of searching and becoming themselves that built his teaching artistry.

The class was transformative for the students - - many surprised their friends, and parents; most of all, they surprised themselves with the discoveries of what they were capable of as actors and as artistic collaborators. Further still, many activated those inner resources that helped them connect to their courage to take risks to grow as people.

In The Milkcrate Monologues Ron Johnson has created a primary artistic resource that turns the trademark milkcrate of vinyl records on its head and converts it into a platform for young people to find their own voices, speak truths and express ideas. The work resonates with the lived experience of a diversity of urban youth, especially young people of color. Gritty in its honesty and perspective The Milkcrate Monologues honors its roots in the authenticity of expression. This means, language is not sanitized; for some of us, buttons will be pushed and triggers activated.

Educators eager to find material and content that speaks to the concerns and perspectives of young people of color turn to Hiphop to provide that relevance and engagement. Too often, however, there is a shallow appreciation for the energy invoked–and they find themselves rushing back to the constraints of conventional propriety and compliance in an effort to put the genie back in the bottle.

Should this be the case, the nation's thought leader on teaching artistry (and fellow actor), Eric Booth, offers useful advice:

> *Give full open, active attention [to the work] - "It is a skill to be able to set aside preconceptions, reactive impulses, and a jumpy mind to fully open one's attention to listening - and one also needs to persist."*
>
> **–Eric Booth in *The Music Teaching Artist's Bible***

While Booth is referring to habits of mind to engage when listening to a piece of music, the approach applies well to encountering any work of art.

And so, I am reminded of a moment of reflection during that first Hiphop theater course when Ron shared, "I don't believe in bad words." Words are universes in themselves that reveal context, feelings, perspective, values, nuance. The Milkcrate Monologues seeks to reflect faithfully its particular universe. As in any work of art, the aim is to communicate ideas with intention as to the form and content that, together, make meaning and express a truth with impact. As you encounter The Milkcrate Monologues you are invited to take Booth's approach and embrace discovery as a creative act. Equip students with the tools to discover their own connections to The Milkcrate Monologues. Focus on the kinds of questions they ask themselves as they engage with it. It is the quality of the questions asked that will yield the deepest insights and discoveries. In this way, students will embark on a rewarding journey to develop their individual voice, perspective and skills as artists and as human beings.

Lilia Agüero
Director of Education
School of Arts and Culture
April 2018

RAP IS NOT MUSIC.

I agree that this must seem like a strange proclamation coming from a long-time practitioner of the craft such as myself but it's true. Yes, Rap can be musical, but many of its most compelling moments have come from a place of non-musicality.

Rap is perhaps the most powerful form of prose known to humankind. Rap's literal sensibility combined with syncopation and rhyme allow the craft to have a resonance that exists outside the realm of what we know as music.

A singer has to approach their subject with poetic flair. Weaving in and out of double entendre and metaphor to make their point. Rap, which in my elder's vernacular simply meant "talk", powers through artifice and delivers a message up close and personal. Now you may not dig said message (and sometimes that's the whole point.) but you are seldom confused about what the message is. With its prose-on-steroids power, Rap has become a weaponized form of personal narrative.

Rap is the go-to form of expression for the marginalized in our society for a reason. Corporate America also understands the power of Rap as a message delivery system and has co-opted it to pitch products and brands.

What does any of the above have to do with the text at hand? Well, the Milkcrate Monologues are a representative slice of the multiplicity of narratives and messages that can be delivered through the rap form. Ron Johnson Jr. a.k.a Philasifer takes us through several tropes and first-person perspectives both common and uncommon within the Rap canon.

Oh, and a few words about theatre. Unlike Mr. Johnson I am not a theatre professional or aficionado (I like what I like). What I can say in the few instances I have seen the worlds of theatre and Rap collide I have been underwhelmed. The creators of the work make a critical mistake by swapping in Rap like it were fodder for a musical. As I have stated, **RAP IS NOT MUSIC.** Using it as just a hip update on the musical form strips the power and authenticity that Rap has.

As a longtime practitioner of the craft, Ron gets this, and The Milkcrate Monologues are not posited as a quirky hybrid but a true Hiphop Theatre (Hiphop capitalized and in front of the word theatre).

In closing, I'd like to give context about the cultural moment that Ron and I come from. In the early to late 90's (for me early for Ron late) there was an emergent subculture within Hiphop culture which is best referred to as "Backpack Rap." This countercultural movement catalyzed by West Coast innovators like the Freestyle Fellowship, Hieroglyphics, and Living Legends, created a visual and sonic aesthetic that ran contrary to the commercialized urban "gangster tropes." Within this moment the Rap narrative broadened and the "regular guy", donning a Jansport Backpack, was given a voice in this new and exciting way. For youth coming up in the semi-suburban trappings of San Jose, California this new wave was very appealing.

A key part of the "Backpack" aesthetic was the milk crate. This is where the medicine men (and women) in Hiphop culture carried their spells (i.e., 12-inch vinyl). Rap is an art form created from the discarded remnants of pop culture and so it is deliciously ironic that a discarded item like a milk crate would be the holder of the disparate sounds that underpin this culture. That's why The Milkcrate Monologues is such an apt metaphor.

Demone Carter
Founder/Director
FutureArtsNow!
April 2018

AUTHOR'S INTRODUCTION

AS I REFLECT ON HIPHOP AS A PREVALENT SUBCULTURE

In its 40th year of existence, I am reminded of many things. How the culture touched my life at a young age, how I watched the culture infiltrate every corner of mass media, fashion, dance, and popular music, and eventually after reaching mainstream status, to slowly become a cliche of itself. As with all things, the more iterations something generates, the more diluted it becomes. I suppose the raw visceral nature of Hiphop and its origins could never truly remain 100% pure.

I feel however as though we have lost so much of the culture to commercialism that we are almost unrecognizable to the originators of the art.

Is it because of the subject matter in Rap? Not really. We've always had a plethora of subjects and styles from the lewd to the truly enlightening.

Is it because of the monetization of the culture? I don't think it's that either. Hiphop from the beginning was big business not only to its practitioners but also to the companies and businesses that were willing to take a chance on it in its inception. (Adidas owes us a lot of money)

It's not the way we present ourselves. it's not that we sign big contracts and forget about our neighborhoods (although those could be contributing factors).

It's the way we allow entities outside of the culture to "SELL" our culture back to us. They take our slang, style, and traditions and then have the audacity to try to program us with it.

TO TRY TO TELL US WHAT THE TRENDS ARE.

They pluck us from our humble beginnings, infuse us with material excess, and feed us suggestions that we then feed to later generations.

THERE WAS A TIME WHERE WE SET THE TRENDS, NOT THEM.

The Milkcrate Monologues is the Lyrical reflection of thoughts on life, hopes, dreams, failures, and triumphs told through the chosen communication medium of Hiphop, Rap.

Hiphop Theatre is a relatively new concept, so in a way, You and I are creating a trend. A format. A mechanism to deliver Hiphop culture through its own traditions without a middleman.

Milkcrate has no Music or Instrumentals. Yet it has a Rhythm. Milkcrate has no trappings of the entertainment industry. yet it seeks to influence and challenge the perceptions of your mind.

I am dedicated to bringing the concept of Rap and Hiphop to you as you've never heard, read, or experienced before.

If the beginnings of the culture we celebrate are any indication, then we'll be in good company.

Ron Johnson Aka PHILASIFER
Author of The Milkcrate Monologues

CHECK THE TECHNIQUE

OK, SO HERE'S HOW THIS WORKS:

I wrote these Hiphop Monologues to be **Studied**, **Rehearsed**, and **Performed**, in front of a class, a workshop, or as auditions for theatre programs. Videos are ok too...

You may do this for free. As long as I am cited and credited as the author. Ron Johnson Jr. or my longtime Rap Alias "**PHILASIFER**" (PHILA - CYPHER) will do. By the time you read this, I will also have an adapted play version of Milkcrate as well. To use that, would require licensing the rights.

If you are unsure about credit for your particular use, consult the information on the copyright page of this book to contact me. I WILL respond.

In this format, not only have I written the monologues, I have also cited all of my influences and references that I use in my verses directly after the monologue itself. A sort of "RAP CLIFF NOTES" if you will...

(I should probably copyright that too)

So not only do you get a feel for how the monologue should come across, but I actually tell you WHY I Wrote it in the first place. You now have everything you need. I look forward to one day hearing and seeing what you do with them.

SIFER

MILKCRATE # 1

"DON'T GIVE ME THAT WEAK SHIT"

WAIT ...(*beat*) I SAID HOLD UP!...(*beat*) Hold Up. Don't give me that WEAK Shit. I SAID: **Don't give me that weak SHIT.**

Don't give me that weak shit, give me that UNIQUE shit, give me that Intriguing, full of meaning human being shit. Intelligence with relevance, some hardness and some elegance to have me eating what you drop from mouth like we were pelicans. I said, don't give me that WEAK SHIT. Give me that supreme SHIT, give me that "wanna-conquer-my-fears-And-live-my-dreams-SHIT." I want that John Lennon, Marvin Gaye, Sinatra, Billie Holiday, Michael Jackson presence that remains and never fades away.

I don't want to hear about your bar drink of choice or sexual exploits or how you did a bid in the pen for trying to help your boys. That shit is old, that shit is cold, that shit is not funny or cute and it damn sure ain't productive and doesn't further my goals. Your gun is not your voice. Your situation was probably not your choice, but your pain can be your power if you give thanks and rejoice. Instead, you exploit and complain you avoid and rearrange like you can invoice people's lives then make 'em charge it to the game--With no respect, accountability, feeling or any shame--and you can bank on industry and the money to be the same--meanwhile, your lame raps influence these young cats to take gaps in education while loading their next gat, cause in *their* world a book is *useless*

UNLESS it's hiding a strap and doctor or lawyer is what they see if they get charged or capped. Tell *us* about how to get free, or how to raise their seed, or how to stop runnin' streets profiled by police, or how to turn a thug life into a positive *at least* and you can start by telling truth and stop perpetuating greed. And that's what I mean when I say: **DON'T GIVE ME THAT WEAK SHIT!**

Give me that *pristine* shit. Give me that in-my-culture-I-still-want-to-*believe* shit. I want that Public Enemy, KRS, Common Sense, Mos Def, Mellie Mel *"The Message"* I can feel the sentence in my chest. MC Lyte, Queen Latifah, Lauryn Hill, Jean Grae, Tupac, Biggie, Big L, with some Mac Dre, Talib Kweli, Del The Funky Emcee, Hieroglyphics, Living Legends Slum Vill and Dubb C, Ice Cube, ZION I, BONE THUGS WITH SOME TRIBE, BLACK MOON ROUND THAT OUT WITH SOME RUN DMC! (beat)

Maybe some Jay-Z . (beat)

Oh. Y'all thought I was done? Soul Sonic Force, The Roots, Lateef Who Speaks the Truth, Gift Of Gab, Aceyalone and the Project Blowed Crew Busta-Bust, Lyrics Born, Beastie Boys, Onyx, Wu-Tang Clan, I give a fuck about what's playing on the radio or what's in demand. **DON'T GIVE ME THAT WEAK SHIT**.

Because people are hurting. People are rich, people are poor, people are working, but they are still human beings and they're deserving. And, Hiphop means intelligent movement, it's *our* tool, we have a duty to not turn the next generation into buffoons. And, if we do... if what racist people say is true... if we took what was once an uplifting culture and medium and let it degrade our world's view, if we let the least intelligent of us speak for us and define rules, if we completely allow the companies to co-op our style, dress, speech, dance, and in return give us inferior versions to sell and program kids on TV telling them what's cool. Then I will gather the righteousness of 400 years of involuntary poverty and anguish as my proof, over two decades of equality and civil rights roots, over 30 years of mainstream stereotype and institutionalized racist abuse, and 40 years' worth of 16 bar verses and inner truth and I will raise my finger, point it, and BLAME *YOU*. For giving me that **WEAK SHIT**.

HIPHOP THAT INSPIRED THIS PIECE

LISTEN

The Revolution will not be televised - Gil Scott-Heron

Scott-Heron, Gil, et al. "The revolution will be jazz: the songs of Gil Scott-Heron - The Revolution will not be televised."

N*ggas Are Scared Of Revolution - The Last Poets

Hendrix, Jimi, et al. "The very best of the Last Poets - Niggas are scared of Revolution."

Award Tour - A Tribe Called Quest

A Tribe Called Quest. "Hits, rarities & remixes - Award Tour."

Move Somethin' - Talib Kweli

Talib Kweli. "Rawkus 2000 New York independent hip hop mixed by Shortee Blitz - Move Somethin."

Re-Definition - BlackStar

Black Star. "Mos Def & Talib Kweli are Black Star - Re:Definition."

We don't Care - Kanye West

Kanye West. "The college dropout."

Black Moon - I Gotcha Open

Black Moon. "Enta da stage." I Got Cha Opin

KRS ONE - The Emcee

KRS-ONE. "Retrospective." The MC

Deception - Blackalicious

Blackalicious, Lateef the Truthspeaker & Cut Chemist. "A2G EP." Deception

WATCH

The Warriors. Paramount Pictures, 1979. Hill, Walter, director. Cyrus' Speech

School Daze. Columbia Pictures, 1988. Lee, Spike, director . Ending sequence of the film.

THEATRE THAT INSPIRED THIS PIECE:

Shakespeare, William. "The Tragedy of Hamlet, Prince of Denmark." *Hamlet, Act III, Scene 2 :|: Open Source Shakespeare*, Open Source Shakespeare, George Mason University., 2003.

Shakespeare, William. "As You Like It." *As You Like It, Act II, Scene 7 :|: Open Source Shakespeare*, Open Source Shakespeare, George Mason University., 2003.

RHYME AND REASON

This is basically the manifesto of the hard-core, no filter, dedicated Hiphop patron who is sick of the culture being used for profit without acknowledging *all* of the value the art possesses. Many years of our music being compromised by corporate interest has left the style of music diluted, a now disrespectful mockery or cliché of itself. To say "**Don't Give Me That Weak Shit**" means that we, Hiphop, as a cultural movement will not stand for anything less than true unadulterated free expression within all the disciplines of Hiphop. Not just the musical form.

MILKCRATE # 2

"LOVE, OR SOMETHING LIKE IT" (F.F.F/K.T.T)

Baby, it's time we tell the truth. It took time for me to be man enough to look you in the face and tell you. It's been happening for a while, I know I feel and so do you that this whole thing has run its course I have no choice, so what's the use.

We're either fussin' or we're fightin' or fuckin' but we ain't loving. And, that's a shame because from you I really wanted something more. We're either kissin' or we're touchin' or trippin' but we ain't trusting. And, we seem to only be concerned with who is keepin' score. It wasn't like that before...

I should have left you/when I meant to/but I was so caught up in you that I could not discern my truth or even look into a mirror and see myself or point of view. At first it was sort of cool, I really felt like we were one until I realized self opinions are not your idea of fun. You had a certain walk, a certain smile, a certain kiss, a certain style, And if I don't adhere to how you vibe it's like you disregard my entire life. And that's hurtful because I liked you for who you were. Our passionate exchanges all a blur, all I remember now is how you made my name a sort of slur. Our relationship covered in mist, not seen but feelings still persist and honestly, if you told me to come to bed now I probably would. My muscle memory senses your touch and even now I feel the rush of what we once were misleading but my ignorance was lush. It's funny how the moments of lust overtake. How the bonds of physicality so easily break, with no foundation, understanding, or empathy in its place, I'm at a dinner table sharing food with an empty space. But not today.

I won't play fast and loose/it's easy to blame you but I must also admit and own up to my part too. I fought you. Maybe I bought you, maybe I wined and dined and stayed blind to what my thoughts do. Maybe I wanted it so bad I played some cards I never had and acted out a play in my brain that wouldn't make you mad. I guess you were what I was supposed to have. Not what I wanted. And now I make excuses and you wonder where my heart went/because I'm not the same man that held your hand and made you promises and even though I'm letting go I swear I always tried to honor them but...

We're either fussin' or we're fightin' or fuckin' but we ain't loving. And, that's a shame because from you I really wanted something more. We're either kissin' or we're touchin' or trippin' but we ain't trusting. And, we seem to only be concerned with who is keepin' score. It wasn't like that before...

Isn't it funny how we always fight after we make love? Because our bodies and our minds trust each other to bring it up. To go back and forth on the things that we never said I think that's when we show feeling and we're really honest enough. Or maybe that's just the buzz. (beat) I laid alone in my room while you'd go clubbin' with your friends, I stared at the wall, wondering how I could make amends and it wasn't until I retraced my steps, that I remembered what I had left. So on our anniversary, I returned to where we first met, saw a woman's locked step, called her over, smiled and offered to pick up her check. And, without warning I told her how I felt. We sat down and I explained to her I needed to start over. No book advice, no counseling, no roll of dice or cried shoulders. I'm not here to blame or call names or tell you what there is to gain, my only interest is that I atone for the pain that I gave. And, then the magic we both gave up on re-appeared. She put her hand in mine, now we exist without time, and I can't call it a relationship, but it might be something like it, more deep, more inclusive, more useful and more inviting.

Now we ain't just fussin' or fighting or fucking because we're loving and, we can't wait to see in each-other's eyes what's in store. Because we're kissing and we're tellin', not trippin' because we're trusting. And, we're not really concerned who's actually keeping score. It's not like before, it's something more...

HIPHOP THAT INSPIRED THIS PIECE

LISTEN

Common. "I Used To Love H.E.R." *Resurrection*, Battery Studios (Chicago), Illinois.

Common. "Come Close." *Electric Circus*, Electric Lady Studios, New York.

Method Man. "Break Ups 2 Make Ups." *Tical 2000: Judgement Day*, The Hit Factory, New York.

2Pac. "Do For Love." *R U Still Down? (Remember Me).*

Lauryn Hill. "Ex - Factor." *The Miseducation of Lauryn Hill.*

Reflection Eternal. "Love Language." *Train of Thought.*

WATCH

West, Kanye . "Def Poetry Jam ." *Def Poetry Jam*, episode Kanye West, Bittersweet, 2005.

THEATRE THAT INSPIRED THIS PIECE

Miller, Arthur. *After the Fall.* New York: Penguin Random House LLC, 2015. eBook.

Miller, Arthur. *A View From The Bridge.* New York: Penguin Random House LLC, 2009. eBook.

Kushner, Tony. *Angels In America.* New York: Theatre Communications Group, Inc., 2013. eBook

Wilson, August. *Fences. New* York: Samuel French, Inc., 1986. Play

Williams, Tennessee. *Cat On A Hot Tin Roof.* New York: New Directions, 1955. eBook

RHYME AND REASON

Although there is a lot of homage to many tortured theatrical relationships in this piece, I draw mostly from my own experience in this. I feel that sometimes, a relationship that is failing needs to fail in order to become something greater. Some of the greatest learning that can be done in a failure is to go back to the beginning and reassess what went wrong, and maybe find some things that were already wrong to begin with. Relationships I believe are no exception.

MILKCRATE # 3

"MARCHING TO NOWHERE"

I'm a soldier. One of fortune or foreclosure. One of fame and exposure, one of the untamed evil vultures that'll swoop on your corpse if it will make me seem bolder. I got the freshest kicks, the dopest whip, the Illest gear and the baddest chick and I know everything it takes to keep this shit. Maybe one day, I'll be able to look into a mirror and say I'm rich enough to be rich. But, until then...

I'm lacin' up my boots with my version of the truth and I'm marchin' to nowhere, marchin' to nowhere. Destroying everything I touch just to get a little rush wish I did but I don't care, did but I don't care.

I know you've seen me homie. I know you wanna BE ME homie. I know you want a taste of that unchecked greed that seems to breed in my semen homie. And you'll wanna be like my kids too, pass the money to these tots they'll be celebrities before they can even develop thoughts and you'll be in the same place you were scrounging for what we drop on the floor. I'm materialistic, you shouldn't be shocked. I got it coming out my ass I'm wiping it with my stocks. Find my crooked cooked books I'm liable to have you shot. I get government subsidies for my friends and me to shop, get a million dollar cut from cartels from you smokin' pot.

That's real for me, happiness is just a dollar bill to me. I spend it with no consequence cause morals don't appeal to me. Morals are for the people who are broken and not equal to superior people like me who never had to work for shit. My father started up this shit, my mother never taught me shit, they gave me money, I watched what they did, and then I copied shit. Because my family name, they still treat me all the same, I could just kill a scientist and supply myself with some brains. If I want it, I have it, If you got it, I'll get it. Leave you crying on 60 minutes and the world will know who did it. You're a pawn, you're a stepping stone, I'll keep you in the back and forth like metronomes, your money's gone I'd teach you to ball but, I work alone.

I'm lacin' up my boots with my version of the truth and I'm marchin' to nowhere, marchin' to nowhere. Destroying everything I touch just to get a little rush wish I did but I don't care, did but I don't care.

I never had love, all I had was stickups and sell drugs, from the hood, told em I'd never forget where I came from. That was until the spotlight, the money, the fame, the honeys, the paparazzi, the people sayin' that they love me. Fuck a community. What did that shit ever do for me? The only way I got out was imitating my TV. I can't go back cause the second I show up they'll kill me! Take my shit and perpetuate the cycle. No mother, no father, no rules but survival so this Hollywood rich shit is just a holiday. Don't care what I gotta do, don't care what I gotta say, don't care what it means to YOU, cause I'm the one that's getting paid, suck my dick if you don't feel me cause that's how it's gonna stay.

I'm lacin' up my boots with my version of the truth and I'm marchin' to nowhere, marchin' to nowhere. Destroying everything I touch just to get a little rush wish I did but I don't care, did but I don't care.

I'm a working class Joe, from a working class home. Stretched my dollars, start a business is my vision. My brother went to college and cheated the market; now he's in prison. My daughter's favorite rapper says it doesn't matter how I get it. But, my parents told me values are the things that make us different. And, I like my hometown, I like helping people, I think the hard work is always what makes us equal but I can't help but think that my ideas aren't in sync with what is going on around me like I'm circling a sink. Because no matter how I soldier, I just can't move boulders that were placed in my way and my kids are just getting older. My hands start to shake but I never tell a doctor cause I'm savin' my dough I need to work to be a good father. And, just once I wish that I was rich and wish it all away, but these cats I see on TV all just seem a little fake. I wonder what their mothers and fathers would say.

I'm on my knees to pray every night I'm seeking grace, but these prayers won't keep the lights on so each and every day I'm lacin' up my boots with my version of the truth and I'm marchin' to nowhere, marchin' to nowhere. I'm losing all my dreams while these others get ahead, wish they did but they don't care, did but they don't care...

HIPHOP THAT INSPIRED THIS PIECE:

LISTEN

Love's Gonna Get'Cha - KRS-One

KRS-One. (1990). Love's Gonna Get'Cha (Material Love). On *Edutainment - Boogie Down Productions*[MP3]. Pal Joey.

My Theme - Nos LeRatZ

Franks, J. (2005). My Theme (Nos LeRatZ). On *Don't Drink the Kool-Aide*[MP3]. Pill Crow's Nest Studios: Nos LeRatz. (2005)

Shook Ones Part II - Mobb Deep

H., & P. (1995). Shook Ones Part II. On *The Infamous..Mobb Deep.*[MP3]. Battery Studios (NYC).

The Rape Over - Yasiin Bey

Bey, Y. (2004). The Rape Over. On *The New Danger*[MP3]. Kanye West.

Train of Thought - Reflection Eternal, DJ Hi Tek, Talib Kweli

Cottrell, T. Kweli, T. (2000). Train of Thought.[MP3]. Rawkus Records.

Stan - Eminem

E., Herman, P., & D. (2000). Stan. On *The Marshall Mathers LP*[MP3]. Eminem & DJ Mark the 45 King.

Money, Power & Respect - The Lox

Kim, L., D., S., J., & Louch, S. (1998). Money, Power & Respect. On *Money, Power & Respect*[MP3]. Jay Garfield, Ron "Amen-Ra" Lawrence, Deric "D-Dot" Angelettie.

Mind Playing Tricks on Me - Getto Boys

King, D., G., W., & S. (1991). Mind Playing Tricks on Me. On *We Can't Be Stopped*[MP3]. Scarface.

10 Crack Commandments - Notorious B.I.G.

Premier, D., & B.I.G., T. N. (1997). 10 Crack Commandments. On *Life After Death*[MP3]. Daddy's House Recording Studios (New York, NY): DJ Premier.

Practice Lookin' Hard - E40

E. (1993). Practice Lookin' Hard. On *The Mail Man*[MP3]. The Mob Shop: Studio Ton.

WATCH

Bamboozled

Lee, S. (Director), & Lee, S. (Writer). (2001). *Bamboozled*[Video file]. USA: New Line Cinema, 40 Acres and a Mule Filmworks.

Juice

Dickerson, E. R. (Director), & Dickerson, E. R. (Writer). (1996-2018). *Juice* [Video file].

New Jack City

Peebles, M. V. (Director). (1991). *New Jack City* [Video file]. USA: Warner Bros.

Do The Right Thing

Lee, S. (Director), & Lee, S. (Writer). (1989). *Do the right thing* [Video file]. USA: Universal.

Wall Street

Stone, O. (Director). (1987). *Wall Street* [Video file]. USA: Twentieth Century Fox.

The Boiler Room

Younger, B. (Director), & Younger, B. (Writer). (2000). *Boiler Room* [Video file]. USA: New Line Cinema.

White Man's Burden

Nakano, D. (Director). (1995). *White Man's Burden*[Video file]. USA: Savoy Pictures.

THEATRE THAT INSPIRED THIS PIECE

Othello ~ Character of Iago

Shakespeare, William . "Othello." *The Tragedy of Othello, Moor of Venice :|: Open Source Shakespeare* , George Mason University.

Tony ~ West Side Story

Laurents, Arthur, et al. "West Side Story.", Heinemann Educational Publishers.

Brother ~ Raisin in The Sun

Hansberry, Lorraine. "A Raisin in the Sun.", Knopf Doubleday Publishing Group.

Biff Loman ~ Death Of A Salesman

Miller, Arthur . "Death of a Salesman.", Penguin Books, Penguin Random House.

RHYME AND REASON

In this piece, I seek to start a dialogue about income disparity, greed, excess morality and values, and most of all, the perceptions associated with these things. To attempt to achieve this, I wrote the monologue perspective from the position of three very distinct angles from various tropes: the legacy rich kid turned businessman, who sees power and privilege as their divine right; the rags to riches entertainer, plucked from obscurity, and pushed into the limelight to be a tool of companies and greed, sacrificing their own standards and way of life to become a stereotype, hand crafted to be sold to others as authentic; the everyman caught in between everything with what appears to be no way out, having none of the advantages that the other two possess, and also none of the baggage. How does the third archetype survive, when these other two tropes are in a struggle for supremacy, and the third just wants to find a way to live in peace? How do WE get to just BE?

MILKCRATE # 4

"THE INFINITE"

It may not be clear, but when you look at me,
I'm not just what you see.
In fact, this shell is a carefully crafted image
to disguise all my ferocity.
You see my true form is infinite and, if I spoke my native
tongue it would explode your head but,
even more so your temperament.
I reincarnate every hundred years to boost morale and,
quell the fear to deconstruct and
reconstruct the very world I engineered.
Some people call me Jesus, some call me Satan but, that's
really just an example of their prejudice interpretation.
Come on.
Let's face it.
I'm a being of knowledge and wisdom dude.
I don't carry the frailty that you humans all
keepin' inside of you.
I was married to Alexandria, the library in Egypt too,
the blacksmith of Zeus's lightning bolt the trusted friend of
Veritas goddess of truth.
I wiped the slate clean in Europe,
they called me bubonic disaster.
Wrote plays and poems in the mid age with Shakespeare,
he's still my favorite rapper.

I brought pain and shallow graves to plantation slave masters
and, gave the white the understanding of black directly after.
If you existed like this,
in these ages upon which I reminisce,
then you would subsequently take every degrading practice
in this current global society as a diss.
So, I can't help but remind you who I am,
I don't have a plan I am the plan
beyond human understanding and,
far from the petty rocks you hold and throw from your hands.
I won your war's, gave you prosperity,
you use it for commercial fluff,
I gave you wealth,
abundant health, for some of you it wasn't enough.
I gave you Elvis's curl and James Brown splits and whirls ,
Jackie's flips,
Michael's angelic voice, and you left them all disturbed.
While I was at that,
I gave you economic boom,
Civil Rights,
Internet, funny cartoons,
safe sex,
you can't sing, I gave you auto tune.

And, even after all that my credibility you try to bruise.
But, if you only knew... that your very primordial
essence is within my grip,
If I spoke the true meaning of the universe your consciousness
and head would split, if I told you that your whole life was the
sum of an equation with skill I conjured with my script and, at

any moment I could erase your thought, identity, possessions and livelihood with the infinite cosmic power at my fingertips.
So, my friend.
I think before you pray to me for another raise or a house and Mercedes Benz,
I think it's time you actually realized exactly.
Who.
You.
Are.
FUCKING WITH!

HIPHOP THAT INSPIRED THIS PIECE

LISTEN

The Story (Ultimate Sacrifice) - Raiderz Of The Lost

Raiderz Of The Lost. "The Story (Ultimate Sacrifice)." *Prepare 4 for Tha Spillage.*

Basic Instructions Before Leaving Earth - Gza

Killah Priest. "B.I.B.L.E. (Basic Instructions Before Leaving Earth)." *Liquid Swords*, RZA's Basement Studio, Staten Island, NY.

I'ma Show 'em - G.R.I.T.S

Grits. "Ima Showem."*Grammatical Revolution.*

Time Is Passing - G.R.I.T.S

Grits. "Time Is Passing." Grammatical *Revolution.*

Clockwork - Blackalicious

Blackalicious. "Clockwork." *A2G EP*, The Hut.

Swan Lake - Blackalicious

Blackalicious. "Swan Lake." *Melodica EP.*

Back to the Essence - Blackalicious

Blackalicious. "Back to the Essence." *A2G EP,* Pajama Studios.

First In Flight - Blackalicious

Blackalicious. "First In Flight ." *Blazing Arrow.*

NoWhere Fast - Blackalicious

Blackalicious. "Nowhere Fast ." *Blazing Arrow.*

Umi Says - Yasiin Bey

Yasiin Bey. "Umi Says ." *Black on Both Sides.*

Judo Flip - Asheru (Boondocks Theme)

Asheru. "Judo Flip."

Poe Man's Dreams (His Vice) - Kendrick Lamar

Kendrick Lamar. "Poe Man's Dreams (His Vice)." *Section.80.*

Cut You Off (To Grow Closer) - Kendrick Lamar

Kendrick Lamar. "Cut You Off (To Grow Closer)." *Overly Dedicated.*

WATCH

Dogma

Smith, Kevin, director. *Dogma.* Lions Gate, 1999

The Last Temptation of Christ

Scorsese, Martin, director. *The last temptation of Christ.* Universal, 1988.

Oh God!

"Oh God!" Warner Home Video, 2002.

Oh God! Book II

Cates, Gilbert, director. *Oh God! Book II*. 1980.

Oh God! You Devil!

Bergman, Andrew. *Oh, God! you Devil*. Warner Bros., 1984.

Defending Your Life

Brooks, Albert, director. *Defending your life*. Warner Bros., 1991.

Phenomenon

Turteltaub, Jon, director. *Phenomenon*. Buena Vista Pictures, 1996.

Kpax

Softley, Iain, director. *K-PAX*. Universal Pictures, 2001.

The Sixth Sense

Shyamalan, M. Night, director. *The Sixth Sense*. Buena Vista Pictures Distribution, 1999.

The Seventh Seal

Bergman, Ingmar, director. *The Seventh Seal*. Svensk Filmindustri, 1956.

THEATRE THAT INSPIRED THIS PIECE

Angels In America ~ Tony Kushner

Kushner, Tony. *Angels In America*. New York: Theatre Communications Group, Inc., 2013. eBook

RHYME AND REASON

Personally, I have always had a hard time internalizing and following religious narratives. I grew up going to Catholic school, learning the customs and tradition, memorizing bible verses, and studying theology on my own. The older I got, the more familiar all of the stories of religion from all over the world sounded, even though they were from different religions and different settings. This led me to my own beliefs that everyone has it right, just in bits and pieces. I wrote this piece from the perspective of a mythological deity. One I believe encompasses all of human history and what it would be like if the being presented themselves to you and spoke.

In rap form of course...

MILKCRATE # 5

"80 LIFE"

They say with each generation something gained, something lost. For me it drifted somewhere between Atari joysticks and 100% cotton striped tube socks. Can't convince me that sh*t didn't pop like multi-colored sugar rock, my generation's last two generations wanna copy off. The music and the dress, the toys and the whims, the culture and the colors, man, you had to be there just to know how it feels. I could use every word I know and still I couldn't make it real. It went so quick like Magic Johnson passes missed the ball on film. And only 80's kids get that reference, time travel and trapping ghosts on my bucket checklist. Moonwalking on my recess break for tips, Hammer pants, British Knights and them sugar high, oversized retro pixie sticks! Now that's what I'm talkin' bout homie! Domino's pizza discount droppin' off Saturday and Sunday quarter stacking arcades like a boss, on my Zack Morris making time freeze as I please tryin' to explain the finer points of this nostalgic scene.

I also remember how close my family was. The nights we ate together, only time I really felt like my kinship was special. I remember every purchase, every time I felt nervous, cause my parents showed me togetherness but never taught me how to preserve it. And now I know what we're missing. We had devices, technological vices that as we grew older took new meaning. The world got colder, the opportunists became bolder and made us think that the material excess of the 80's our parents had was what we were seeking. So, we built shrines to celebrity, left out the levity, focused on the payday and downgraded integrity. What's missing is the happiness and a step with a spring, what's missing is the joy of play and not all the things, what's missing is the people you were with and shared the gift of laughter and companionship.

But, today's friends are tomorrow's competitors. Today's lens is tomorrow's post editor. I wish that sometimes I could go back to 1989 and screw adolescence and adulthood altogether. But, as a child of the 80's I'm just thankful that it made me, cause the skinny jeans and shit that y'all be rockin is just crazy...

HIPHOP THAT INSPIRED THIS PIECE

LISTEN

Back in the day - Ahmad
Ahmad. "Back in the day ." *Ahmad.*

Do You Remember ? - The Last Emperor
The Last Emperor. "Do You Remember?" *Hidden Treasures.*

Seasons - Cunninlyguists Feat. Masta Ace
Cunninlyguists Feat. Masta Ace. "Seasons."

Time Machine - Sweatshop Union
Sweatshop Union. "Time Machine." *Water Street.*

Living Legends - Classic
Living Legends. "Classic." *Classic.*

Toy Jackpot - Blackalicious
Blackalicious. "Toy Jackpot."

Santa's Rap - Beat Street Soundtrack

Treacherous Three. "Xmas Rap." The *Sugar Hill Records Story.*

WATCH

80's The Decade That Made Us - National Geographic

Nutopia. "80's The Decade That Made Us - National Geographic." *80's The Decade That Made Us* , season 1, episode 1, National Geographic, 2013.

The Eighties - CNN

Season 1, CNN, 2016.

The Back To The Future Film Series (1985-1990)

Zemeckis, Robert, director. *Back to the future: the complete trilogy*. Universal Studios, 2010.

The Ghostbusters Film Series (1984-1989)

Reitman, Ivan, director. *Ghostbusters 1 & 2*. Sony pictures home entertainment, 2008.

Magic Johnson: Always Showtime

"Magic Johnson: Always Showtime." NBC Entertainment, 1993.

Michael Jackson: The Magic Continues

"Michael Jackson: The Legend Continues." Showtime Networks, 1992.

Michael Jackson's Moonwalker

"Moonwalker." Warner home video, 2009.

Teenage Mutant Ninja Turtles (1989)

"Teenage Mutant Ninja Turtles." 1987.

Saved By The Bell (TV Show)

Saved By The Bell. Created by Steve Bobrick, NBC.

RHYME AND REASON

I was born in the Eighties. 1983 to be exact. This statement carries with it a whole host of memories, experiences, and emotional attachment that you could only feel if you were actually alive in the decade in which I speak. Culturally speaking, people equate the greatness of the eighties to the music or the technology boom that basically ushered in the renaissance that gave birth to all the things we have today. But what I find interesting is that the generation of kids born in the eighties will forever be the only group who had an analog childhood/ adolescence, and also had a digital adulthood. In this piece I try to capture the sights and sounds, but also try to explain its effect on the family unit, the economy and people's faith in the system, and the erosion and decay of moral values that also made the eighties a special thing to behold, but for a very different reason. It wasn't all neon lasers and leg warmers. But, to be fair there was a lot of that...

"But, sometimes I do sit and reminisce then, think about the years I was raised, back in the day." ~Ahmad

MILKCRATE # 6

"UNTITLED"

What it was, what it is, what it could be. I heard the past bites asses with some sharp teeth. I heard the present has some wonderful lessons if you can catch em and the future isn't clear but we can always correct it.

Looking back for me is painful but for all the wrong reasons. Most of the opportunities that popped up I seized em. What I regret most is not just focusing on one, became a jack of all trades and a master of none. Except for rapping and acting cause I consider them equal sum of all experience and possibility that I've become. But, the brain still wanders. The heart becomes fonder.

I feel as though I have died and been reborn a hundred times on this planet. I've always been a spiritual person. Not in a conventional sense, but I believe that as humans our greatest ability and best hope for the future lies in our ability to understand our failures or misdirection, and triumphantly begin anew. I believe that we are living, breathing examples of this to ourselves and to each other. I can only begin with this statement because I feel it necessary to explain to you who I once was, so that you can truly have a clear understanding of who I am.

A child born from love in a world of promise 1983 on The 15th in Steinbeck country Salinas, California. Ever since I was able to comprehend speech, I was an entertainer. A person who seeks joy and fulfillment through the joy of others.

I remember being five years old rehearsing my recitation of Abraham Lincoln's speeches to perform to on-lookers under the shady trees of Casa De Fruta. The time I spent singing and dancing to Michael Jackson cassette tapes in my bedroom, the smell of the stage makeup ever present on my collar during my first stage musical, and the feeling of accomplishment after writing my first rap on a torn notepad.

In fact, ever since I understood the power of words, I have been a writer. A person inspired by the unfamiliar inner workings of the human spirit and propelled by digging in the depths of my vocabulary and personal complexity to try to define it a way no one else can. My poems, my scars, my loves, my Hiphop 16 bars, my own personal freedom for the world to see. It's not about the notoriety, it's just about me.

But, I can't lie that notoriety is not what I seek, in fact my competitive nature once led me to be an athlete. Once a man full of pride, at the free-throw line I would reside on the black-top down the street.

Even now in my mind I hear the crowd roar as I shake the imaginary defenders take a step back and drop into the chain linked hoop what would be considered in the league regulation as a "three". A dedicated player and lover of the game a shame my number or jersey will never be retired or even seen.

But, it's all in me still, it's not a matter of flattery but, really a matter of will and of skill for I can't think of a better way to release all my ills but, to tell you that all of these dreams have been killed. And still there is mourning but, still there is morning! I don't even know you but I want you to smile. I don't know you but I want to challenge your mind. I don't even know you but I want you to challenge mine!

And, the man with the plans who began this has peace.

For I'm not just one of these men, I am all three. And the pieces of all of these deaths create me.

This speech has no title, but if it did, I would call it, belief.

HIPHOP THAT INSPIRED THE PIECE

LISTEN

The Balance - Aceyalone

Aceyalone. "The Balance ." *A Book Of Human Language.*

8 Moons Ago - Camp Lo

Camp Lo. "8 Moons Ago ."*Let's Do it Again.*

Reflect/Connect - Philasifer (Grown Man Mixtape)

Philasifer. "Reflect/Connect." *The Grown Man Mixtape*, 221 B Studios, Tucson, AZ, 2009.

Daylight / Nightlight - Aesop Rock

Aesop Rock. "Night Light." Daylight.

Nights Like This - J-Live

J-Live. "Nights Like This." *All of the Above.*

Worldwide - DJ Jazzy Jeff Feat. Pauly Yams & Baby Blak

DJ Jazzy Jeff. "Worldwide." *The Magnificent.*

40 oz For Breakfast - Blackalicious

Blackalicious. "40oz. for Breakfast." *Melodica EP.*

Whirlwind Thru Cities - Afu Ra

Afu Ra. "Whirlwind Thru Cities ." *Body of the Life Force.*

Tearz - Wu Tang Clan

Wu-Tang Clan. "Tearz." *Enter the Wu-Tang 36 chambers*, Firehouse Studios, Brooklyn, New York, 1992.

If I Ruled The World - Nas

Nas. "If I Ruled the World (Imagine That)." *It was written.*1996.

Pain - 2pac (Above The Rim Soundtrack)

2Pac. "Pain ." *Above the rim: the soundtrack*. 1994.

WATCH

It's A Wonderful Life (1946)

Capra, Frank, director. *It's a Wonderful Life*. RKO Radio Pictures, 1946.

Quantum Leap (TV Series)

Bellisario, Donald P., et al. *Quantum Leap*, NBC.

The Count Of Monte Cristo (2002)

Reynolds, Kevin, director. *The Count of Monte Cristo*. Touchstone Pictures, Spyglass Entertainment/Buena Vista Pictures Distribution, 2002.

V For Vendetta (2005)

McTeigue, James , director. *V for Vendetta. V for Vendetta*, Warner Bros. , 11 Dec. 2005.

THEATRE THAT INSPIRED THIS PIECE

Hamlet Act III : Scene I ~ "To Be , Or Not To Be...", Macbeth Act III : Scene II ~ "My Mind's filled with scorpions..."

Shakespeare, William. "Open Source Shakespeare." Edited by Eric Johnson, *Open Source Shakespeare*, Bernini Communications LLC/ George Mason University.

Fences - August Wilson
Wilson, August. *Fences: August Wilson*. Samuel French, 2010.

The Piano Lesson - August Wilson
Wilson, August. *Piano Lesson*. Plume, 1990.

Dreamgirls - Tom Eyen
Krieger, Henry, and Tom Eyen. *Dreamgirls. Music by Henry Krieger. Book and lyrics by Tom Eyen*. Hal Leonard Publishing Corporation, 2007.

The Stronger - August Strindberg
Strindberg, August, et al. *Plays: two*. Methuen Drama, 2000.

RHYME AND REASON

In this piece, I am starting a conversation about personal gain and human experience, accumulated through rejection, loss, defeat and regret. The symbolism is death, but not in the scientific sense: the death of the old ideal as a beginning to a new, far from the baggage and the past expectations of life. When I say I have died a hundred times on this planet, it means I have given up truths in search of the greater truth, letting go of the realities that were proven to be false in my life. We have tried many paths in life and some that began to nurture our existence naturally change into something we hadn't previously expected, and faded away. Some paths we never thought we would take became the path needed to become the people we are, and continue to bear fruit.

"Giving is receiving, seeing is believing,
and the world just rotates so harmonious and even.
It's perfectly balanced..." - **Aceyalone**

MILKCRATE # 7

"SOMEBODY'S GONNA DIE TODAY"

Somebody's gonna die today. Let's hope it's not you or me, cause I got things to do, places to go, people to see. I haven't found the promise of the brighter day in which I seek, I've gotta find my purpose before someone writes my eulogy.

Never enough time, never enough rhyme and never enough effort I could ever put behind me. I'm driven, but what for? I don't have seconds to explore that concept. I'm too busy in a rush to do some more. Can't take time so I can't make time to fear the reaper. I guess time could be money cause I never have either. And that's real like the wrinkles forming on my face. Ignore the pain as I soldier towards the shine of that brighter day. To be unique you have to act on instinct and impulse to do it, and I'm afraid to go to sleep because I feel like one day I will awake and lose it. So, in between the verses I'm a zombie neglecting all my thoughts of self-preservation for the art, and therein lies the irony. If I take this too deep I could further sink my feet into the creeping calculation of our eminent eternal sleep.

Because...

Somebody's gonna die today. Let's hope it's not you or me, 'cause I got things to do, places to go people to see. I haven't found the promise of the brighter day in which I seek, I've gotta find my purpose before someone writes my eulogy. It's a selfish thought. But, we've all had one. Passing by an accident, seeing the carnage and being glad it's not anyone that you love. But, what if it could have been? Someone you would greet, someone you were about to meet, somebody's future wife or mother is mangled in that car seat. Somebody's reason for living, somebody's mission, somebody's only friend in life is about to come up missing. But, for that second we're aware, we pretend not to care but hold our loved ones a little tighter when we finally get there. I don't think that any of us are inevitably prepared to be the one or lose the one that we could never ever bear. And, that fact remains on the ethereal plane cause we couldn't even function with that state of mind day to day. In times of most serious fray, we can acknowledge denial works in mysterious ways.

But...

Somebody's still gonna die today. Let's hope it's not you or me, 'cause I got things to do, places to go people to see. I haven't found the promise of the brighter day in which I seek, I've gotta find my purpose before someone writes my eulogy.

But, if me it is I have to make sure my life is well lived, create a future with a purpose and some choices for my kids. Create a picture of importance other people might outlive with some lasting impressions inspiration might give. Because when it comes to death it immediately becomes a legacy discussion, I want fanfare and assurances that my life ain't for nothing so, even on my deathbed I have to still continue frontin' cause if eternal life is real then I need to start planning something...

HIPHOP THAT INSPIRED THIS PIECE

LISTEN

Payroll Professionals - Pigeon John, Featuring Joey the Jerk & Flynn (Producer)

Pigeon John, "Move On." *Pigeon John is Clueless. 2001*

My Soul On Ice - Ice

Ice-T. "Soul on Ice." *Power.*1988

God's Work - MURS

Murs. "God's Work." *The End of the Beginning.*

C.R.E.A.M - Wu Tang Clan

Wu-Tang Clan. "C.R.E.A.M." *Enter the Wu-Tang (36 Chambers),* Firehouse Studios, Brooklyn, NY.

A Better Tomorrow - Wu Tang Clan

Wu-Tang Clan. "A Better Tomorrow." *Wu-Tang Forever.*

Workin' - PDiddy

Puff Daddy & the Family. "Workin' (Remix)." *MMM (Money Making Mitch).*

Through The Wire - Kanye West

Kanye West. "Through the Wire." *The College Dropout*, The Record Plant, Los Angeles, CA.

Sing About Me (Dying Of Thirst) - Kendrick Lamar

Kendrick Lamar. "Sing About Me, I'm Dying of Thirst." *Good kid, m.A.A.d city,* TDE The Red Room, Carson, CA.

Tried By 12 - East Flatbush Project

East Flatbush Project. "Tried by 12." *First Born: Overdue,* 10/30 Uproar Records, Brooklyn, NYC, NY.

Good Mourning - Reflection Eternal
Reflection Eternal. "Good Mourning." *Train of Thought.*

THEATRE THAT INSPIRED THIS PIECE

Proof (2000) - David Auburn
Jenkins, Jeffrey Eric., et al. *The best plays of 2000-2001.* Limelight editions, 2000.

A Question Of Mercy (1996) - David Rabe
Jenkins, Jeffrey Eric., et al. *The best plays of 2000-2001.* Limelight editions, 2000.

Rent (1996) - Jonathan Larson
Larson, Jonathan. *Rent: the complete book and lyrics of the Broadway musical.* Applause Theatre and Cinema Books, 2008.

RHYME AND REASON

This piece deals with mortality, specifically as it applies to denial, and how as a country, we tend to define ourselves through our pain, suffering and our life's work. This is a retrospective, permeating theme almost through the entire set of monologues. Coincidentally, I had the idea to write these monologues while I was in the ICU of a hospital in Gilroy, California. I, like many people, spent years focused on my life's pursuit of acting and being a musician literally it would seem, almost to the point of death. Neglecting my health, I pursued artistic greatness, completely ignorant of the way my body was breaking down. When I regained consciousness, I remember the first thought I had: "How much longer do I have to be in this bed before I can get up and work again?" I consider this truly shameful, being that the thought of my wife, my family, and my friends remained second. Over the next long 7 days, I realized that I needed to organize my life like I organized my career, and that my family must take priority. Eventually, the planning stopped being about me, and it started being about them. This piece marks the transition of the two for me.

MILKCRATE # 8

"THEY BE ILLIN'"

1986. The golden age of Hiphop as it's written by the spectators and pens. The culture was 7 years old, the little white boy was 10. Father was a musician, bluegrass and rock and roll, but it's a long time since Elvis had the crowds under his control. Something new is taking hold. Something fresh, something bold. Of course I'm speaking of spoken word and looped beats from the ghetto streets and dancing can-sprayin' with that sweet technique! Before the whole country could say *"Rapper's Delight"*, kids in the suburbs was practicing their skills on the mic.

And, he was one of many, tapes of all his favorite rappers he had plenty. The hours spent rehearsing boggled the mind, memorization of the verses were the inertia of this moment in time. That perfect moment, where he has all the right performance components. When he steps on stage of his entire Catholic private school and owns it. The people would cheer he thought, it would be real he thought, at the lunch time cypher session he'd be a big deal! He thought. He had determination, extra poise, extra patience, extra will, stage presence and most of all preparation. His rap debut on stage something they're sure to be feelin' the group: Run-DMC, the song: *"You Be Illin' "*

You know how the track goes, I don't even have to tell you, like the perfect silly rap song he could do at this venue. The irony is It talks about nothin' but people trippin' off of themselves having perceptions on one side when it's really somethin else. And, like I said this is the perfect song that Nuns need to hear. He could have single handedly opened eyes and claimed ears. Could have left the stage praised and respected and revered. Could have paved the way for his entertainment rap career. But, as with life we can prepare, but we cannot predict the seasons, we cannot predict the disappointment, lessons, or the reasons. Or, a little boy's dreams no matter how far or close he gets. How did it go? We'll never know. He was flagged as inappropriate.

Yeah.

And, beating kids with rulers is not.

And, molesting little boys in pews and lying to the Diocese is really what's hot.

Sometimes I wonder how God took it or what Jesus really thought, that day his followers stole a boy's confidence and creative spark.

Or when the people of God claiming to be righteous turn their tolerance off,

And, every second ticking closer to their judgement on the clock.

They probably look down, turn to each other and say: " THEY BE ILLIN'."

HIPHOP THAT INSPIRED THIS PIECE

LISTEN

You Be illin' - Run DMC

Run-DMC. "You be Illin'." *Raising Hell*, Chung King Studios.

Laugh Track - Nos Leratz Feat. Abomb ,Philasifer & No Wonder

Nos Leratz. "Laugh Track." *Don't Drink the Kool-Aide,* Pill Crow's Nest.

THEATRE THAT INSPIRED THIS PIECE

Henry V Act II Scene II ~ Boy's Monologue

Shakespeare, William, and A. R. Humphreys. *Henry V: William Shakespeare*. Penguin Books, 1975.

RHYME AND REASON

This piece, like many of the pieces in this book, is based on a true event, as good raps sometimes should be. However, this story is not my own. It was created based on a story that a longtime friend told me about his experiences in a Catholic school that we both attended as children. At the time, you have to understand that the global force that was the Hiphop sound was literally invading everyone's ear drums. It went from white communities calling it a fad, to it being in national commercials and winning Grammys almost OVERNIGHT. What particularly interested me in his story, was that in his society, he had been shunned and belittled for his interests and affinity, yet a cultural movement created thousands of miles away readily accepted him and gave voice to his art. This speaks to the healing power of Hiphop culture. We became the new Ellis Island for artists that felt they could no longer be understood anywhere else. I have made Hiphop music with this friend of mine for over 14 years. He is by far one of the most gifted lyricists and producers that I have ever seen. Shout out to Nos Leratz!

"To the gifted Nos Leratz! This is dedicated to those that slept in the past..." ~ **Nos Leratz**

MILKCRATE # 9

"POOR MAN'S FRONT DOOR"

Listen. Did you hear that? (beat) I said, did you HEAR THAT? That's the sound of your life, hopes, and dreams ticking away slowly (beat) The small and large hands pass at a snail's pace, when you're lonely. Did you SEE that? (beat) I said, DID YOU SEE THAT? (beat) That's the image of it passing by... (beat) Trying to make sense of it when you're fact-less. Trying to reach your hand out, grab it, and gather it and put it together like change from underneath a sofa or a mattress. But, still it fades...like the sepia glossy shade on the face of a 1940's movie actress. And, in its place: madness. (beat)

What if the poor were actually rich? And, the rich deserved the back entrance? But, we've been raised and socialized to never open our eyes and recognize the difference? Then maybe we wouldn't be in such a hurry to discard our humanity. Maybe we wouldn't be in such a hurry to screw each other to get "rich". Cause it ain't funny being someone else's bitch. (beat) But, the biggest trick the wealthy ever pulled was convincing you that unless you have THINGS, your happiness doesn't exist.

And the second you ever got a clue you'd be off that list. Without a government note in your hand you feel limiTED, but forgot that the number zero is limitLESS. (beat) A broke man believes anything that you tell him, a rich man will buy anything that you can sell him. So, if I told you that prosperity exists inside the soul and not in the expectation of your peers, would you Internalize that? Or, would it be valued by gilded ears?

Only time will tell whether the disenfranchised will explore the true riches of life that await through the poor man's front door. The value of possessions transmuted for the value of truth. The most coveted currency we search for. No less. No more.

HIPHOP THAT INSPIRED THIS PIECE

LISTEN

Fire In The Booth Pt. 1 - Akala

Akala. "Fire in the Booth Pt. 1, 2 & 3." *MOBO.*

Mista Mista - The Fugees

Fugees. "Mista Mista." *The score,* Booga Basement Studio, New Jersey.

Mr. Wendel - Arrested Development

"Mr. Wendel." *Arrested Development.*

Times Square 2:30A.M. (Segue) - Tony Toni Tone

Tony Toni Tone. "Times Square 2:30A.M. (Segue) ."

Paid In Full - Eric B. & Rakim

Eric B. & Rakim. "Paid in Full." *The Best of Eric B. & Rakim*, 7 July 1987.

First Of The Month - Bone Thugs In Harmony

Bone Thugs-n-Harmony. "1st of tha Month." E. 1999 Eternal, Trax Recordings Studio (Hollywood, California), CA.

Livin Life - Athletic Mic League

Athletic MIC league. "1st of tha Month." *Sweats & Kicks.*

That Ain't Love - Little Brother

Little Brother. "That Ain't Love ." *Getback.*

Window Shopper - 50 Cent

50 Cent. "Window Shopper." *Get rich or die tryin music from and inspired by the motion picture.*

Hard Times - Run DMC

Run-D.M.C. "Hard Times." Run-*D.M.C.*, Greene St. Recording.

Spaceship - Kanye West

Kanye West. "Spaceship." The *College Dropout*, Sony Music Studios, NYC and Larrabee Sound North, Los Angeles., CA.

WATCH

With Honors (1994)

Keshishian, Alek, director. *With Honors*. Warner Bros., 1994.

The Five Heartbeats (1991)

Townsend, Robert, director. *The Five Heartbeats* . 20th Century Fox, 1991.

Beat Street (1984)

Lathan, Stan , director. *Beat Street* . Orion Pictures,

Capitalism : A Love Story (2009)

Moore, Michael, director. *Capitalism : A Love Story*. The Weinstein Company, 2009.

The Firm (1993)

Pollack, Sydney, director. *The Firm,* Paramount Pictures, 1993

Mo Money (1992)

Macdonald , Peter, director. *Mo Money,*Columbia Pictures, 1992.

The Pursuit Of Happyness (2006)

Muccino, Gabriele, director. *The Pursuit Of Happyness.* Columbia Pictures, 2006.

THEATRE THAT INSPIRED THIS PIECE

Death Of A Salesman - Arthur Miller

Miller, Arthur . *Death of a Salesman,* Crome Publishing, 2016.

Les Misérables - Claude-Michel Schönberg, Alain Boublil

SCHÖNBERG, CLAUDE-MICHEL, and Alain Boublil. *Les Misérables Songbook,* Hal Leonard Publishing Corporation, 2012.

RHYME AND REASON

(Note : This was originally Written for the soundtrack "Songs Inspired By 7 , 8ight , 9 : A Play written by Joe Luis Cedillo")

Few people have truly explored the depths of poverty. Few people have truly tasted the desperation, the emptiness, or the lasting impacts of being cast out of our social contract and being forced to live below the poverty line or worse, even further below the poverty line. What I propose in this piece is that maybe we have been socialized to value the wrong things in life. In my opinion, people matter. money does not. The true wealth of life rests in the experiences of people. Not money.

Poor man's front door was written to examine the self-induced pain we inflict on ourselves trying to adhere to the purchase of modern status symbols, greed, and disassociation with those who do not subscribe to those principles. And, most importantly, how lonely our consumer culture really is and the depression involved with owning material possessions, but not having anyone to actually share it with. It also examines a certain freedom that we can achieve by casting aside our materialism and seeking the knowledge of others, the beauty of nature, and the joy of mere existence. True value.

"Money is a means to get wealth. Not the wealth itself."

~Akala

MILKCRATE #10

"ROBOTS FOR BREAKFAST 1 & 2"

A SIDE

I activated my power source today at 0-7:0-0. Designation: morning, diagnostic: energy low. Required fuel, initiated the docking sequence with my stove, to ensure the sustenance was not cold. Optical display kinda blurry, still waking up. Reflexive joints on an axis 'till I've stretched enough. Planning my day with cerebral lobe scanners in this technical metropolis that dropped like a hammer on the organic flesh, took society to test, all the limits of our preconceived notions of advanced. Involuntary harmony of man and metal form the best. Evolved being, but we lack the organs in the chest. And, even still my genetic code is restless, optimization of all my feelings in a Google checklist. I'd give my android left arm for an imperfect respite. Only partially human, eating robots for breakfast.

B SIDE

Recharging sequence complete. Redeem my new stomach with a warranty receipt. A door sealed tight with a vertical release, mechanical dog barking stupid algorithm on repeat. Makes it hard to calculate numbers on digital sheep, or what humanoids used to call dozing off to sleep. Absorb my news on a single touch activated sheet on a trackless monorail traveling faster than speech. A future that's advanced but it's far from unique. How many inferior units scrapped at the heap? Organic skin only wins at a slow defeat. Shed a tear for my generation, but it's made of grease. Fleece of gold gleams with nano components but, what good is perfect society if you don't own it? A factory assembled smile placed on your orifice. Encased in a prison that you're programmed not to notice.

So, focus...

HIPHOP THAT INSPIRED THIS PIECE

LISTEN

The 6th Sense - Common Feat. DJ Premier

Common. "The 6th Sense (Something You Feel)." *Like Water for Chocolate*, D&D Studios (New York City), NY.

Can We Auto Correct Humanity? - Prince EA

Prince EA. "Can We Auto Correct Humanity? ." *Can We Auto Correct Humanity? .*

A.D.H.D - Kendrick Lamar

Kendrick Lamar. "A.D.H.D." *Section.80.*

New World Water - Mos Def

Yasiin Bey. "New World Water." *Black on Both Sides.*

Everybody - Logic

Logic. "Everybody." *Everybody*, Logic's Studio.

The Cure - J Cole

J. Cole. "The Cure." *The Cure.*

The Announcement - Jay Electronica

Jay Electronica. "The Announcement." *Jay Electronica.*

Literally Anything Rage Against The Machine

Rage Against The Machine. *Rage Against the Machine.*

WATCH

The Matrix Series (1999-2003)

Brothers, The Wachowski, director. *The Matrix*. Warner Bros. Pictures, 1999.

Johnny Mnemonic (1995)

Longo, Robert , director. *Johnny Mnemonic*. TriStar Pictures, 1995.

Alien Series (1979-Present)

Scott, Ridley, director. *Alien*. 20th Century Fox, 1979.

PI (1998)

Aronofsky, Darren, director. *Pi*. Artisan Entertainment, 1998.

Blade Runner (1982)

Scott, Ridley, director. *Blade Runner*. Warner Bros. Pictures, 1982.

Robocop (1987)

Verhoeven, Paul , director. *RoboCop*. Orion Pictures, 1987.

The Terminator Series (1984-present)

Cameron, James, director. *The Terminator*. Orion Pictures, 1984.

Ghost In The Shell (1995)

Oshii, Mamoru, director. *Ghost In The Shell*. Shochiku, 1995.

Freejack (1992)

Murphy, Geoff, director. *Freejack*. Warner Bros., 1992.

Tron (1982)

Lisberger, Steven , director. Tron. Walt Disney Productions, 1982.

THX 1138 (1971)

Lucas, George, director. *THX 1138*. Warner Bros., 1971.

Metropolis (1927)

Lang, Fritz, director. *Metropolis*. UFA, 1927.

Theatre that Inspired this Piece

Earthquake Sun - Luis Valdez (2004)

Valdez, Luis. "Earthquake Sun." Aug. 2004, San Diego, San Diego Repertory Theatre.

Dynamo - Eugene O'Neill (1929)

O'Neill, Eugene. *Dynamo*. Kessinger Publishing, 2004.

The Adding Machine - Elmer Rice (1923)

Rice, Elmer. *The adding machine*. Diesterweg, 2001.

RHYME AND REASON

This piece is written to assess our relationship in society with technology; its perks, but mostly its flaws. The landscape of ***"Robots for Breakfast"*** exists in a post-apocalyptic utopia (oxymoron intended) from the position of a man who trades pieces of his own body for the "improvements" of technology directly grafted to his flesh. He has done this so often in his life to this point, he can no longer feel what it means to be human. The question is simple I believe: how much of our body, mind and soul will eventually have to be given up for a perfectly connected, non-emotional, instant gratification society? How much have we lost already?